*"Finally a beautifully written, smart and savvy book for all yoga students, instructors, and those who may be interested in yoga. Susan gives ideas not only easy to understand but fantastically creative, just like her!"*
**—Nancy Orlen Weber RN, CCA**

*"As you read through this beautiful book, Susan's loving, bright spirit shines through the pages as if she were right beside you, gently guiding you through the coupling of asana with the frequency of high quality essential oils. This primer provides expert guidance for a yoga practice to effectively evolve into an elevated form."*
**—Gailann Greene Young Living Diamond**

*"Susan provides the inexperienced health seeker an introduction into the world of yoga, then gently interweaves the power of essential oils. The more experienced yoga students will find profound ways to deepen their practice with Susan's step-by-step guide of incorporating essential oils into their asana and meditation practice, and she deftly and compassionately opens the mind of the yoga instructor to the world of financial abundance."*
**—Sue Pelechaty - BS, CCA**

*"Susan is one of the best instructors, mentors, and inspirational leaders I know. This book is like having a class with her everyday!"*
**—Kim Keenan CYI**

# AromaFlow Yoga

## How to Use Essential Oils in your Practice to Manifest Wellness and Prosperity

Susan Santoro Martz

> *"Deep in their roots,*
> *all flowers keep the light"*
> - Theodore Roethke

## DEDICATION

Nothing is ever accomplished without the support of a tribe. Thank you Mom and Dad, without your love of dance (and me), I would never have known the light that sparks me. To my inspiring band of Luminaries, who have shaped who I am as an AromaFlow instructor and team player, it's your light that illuminates my path. For all the leaders who have taught and supported me on my oily path, your mentorship inspires me to step into the brightness of my light. In gratitude of my beautiful sisters who remind me everyday the value of my light. Thank you to Leah, your sense of balance and design illuminates my vision. For my talented niece Janna who said yes to my spark and sprinkled her writers dust all over this book. To my boy Denver who models courage in the face of fear, and reminds me to hit it out of the ballpark, you are the light. And to my hubby Greg, your dedication to uncovering your true light humbles me and I am sparked once again!

For D. Gary Young who's light burned bright in this lifetime. Thank you for igniting the flame that led me to the world of nature's apothocary. 1949-2018

# TABLE OF CONTENTS

# Origins

# SOURCE

I came out of my mother's womb singing and dancing Broadway show tunes, it was in my DNA and a big part of my upbringing. My mom would listen to forties swing music on the radio while packing our school lunches in the morning. She would play the piano during the holidays and my family and I sang-a-long at the top of our lungs. I spent the better part of my youth singing and dancing at local dance schools and watching my mom and dad take to the dance floor at family weddings and anniversaries showing everybody "how it was done." They danced the Lindy, Cha Cha, and Foxtrot, and knew just what step the other was going to take before it was taken. They had a dance language all their own, weaving in and out of each other's arms and feet, while following split second cues with ease and grace. I'd sit at the kid's table watching them with a big ol' grin on my face secretly hoping my dad would extend his hand to me and ask me to dance too . . . he did . . . every time. My parents didn't know it at the time, but they were showing me a joy and aliveness that shaped my destiny for years to come. Even at a young age, moving through space to the rhythm of the music set me free; it altered my reality, and allowed me a deeper connection to my purpose and life. But as a kid, I had no idea that all that shaping and connecting was going on. All I knew was that I wanted to dance.

My dad took me to see my first Broadway show *Pippin*, when I was thirteen. I sat mesmerized on the edge of my seat waiting for the next dance number.

It was then that I realized the magnitude of my desire to dance. I turned to my dad after the show was over and said, "I'm going to do that someday, Dad." Fifteen years later my dad sat in the tenth row of the Wintergarden theatre and watched me perform on Broadway in CATS.

The desire to feel life through movement was at the core of my being. It was exhilarating and very much ALIVE during my twenties and it drove me to live life to its fullest. At the time, it was all so innate. Dancing my way through life wasn't a conscious plan, it was just something I did. Because living without pirouettes, grand jeté, and hitch kicks wasn't an option. The thing is, I thought all that awesome was only found on stage, when I performed.

It wasn't until I took some much needed R&R time away from my performing career that I realized the awesomeness could be found in a more simple and quiet way. I was exhausted from performing eight shows a week. Don't get me wrong, I loved my life in the performing arts, but all those years of push and drive to get myself to the Broadway stage, and keeping up with my peers for ten years at eight shows a week had caught up to me, and I was worn out. Listening to a friend's advice, I took one of my vacation weeks and drove up to a yoga center in Lenox, Massachusetts named Kripalu. Along with massages, facials, and hot saunas, they offered yoga. It was the early nineties, before yoga retreats were the trend, and Kripalu was considered an *ashram,*

so the stigma of communal living had my weird-dar
pinging. Lots of thoughts crossed my mind when
I approached the modest looking former Jesuit
seminary; will I be abducted and will my parents
have to come and do an intervention? Am I stepping
into a cult? Or what if I don't like tofu? My body was
tired and the idea of soothing massages, facials, and
saunas was all I could think of, so I trusted my friend
and made a go of it.

It was my first yoga class in one of the open
spaced rooms when the paradigm shifted for me.
It was early morning, too early for this late night
theatre girl. I found myself flat on the floor, the sun
rising, casting an orange glow in the room. It was
incredibly quiet, except for the lullaby music that
played under the even tones of the instructors voice.
She was guiding the class from one movement to
the next while instructing us to take deep breaths in
and out. Meanwhile I'm thinking, "If things don't pick
up, I'm gonna be nappin' here in a minute." No lights,
orchestra, audience, or make-up. No adrenaline or
anticipatory excitement to set my body in motion. No
sign of an approaching fanfare, it was just me, the
sound of my breath, and the idea that I was ready for
a big ol' nap.

I kept pushing away the sleepies, wanting nothing
more than to check out, let alone follow the teacher's
instructions, "Take a deep breath in, wrap your legs
one over the other, turn your upper body in the
opposite direction, and let your legs fall gently to the

floor." She kept putting me to sleep with her words, "As you let gravity take over . . . release your breath with the sound of ahh." As instructed, I crossed my legs, twisted my spine and played with gravity's opposing pull . . . then it happened. I released my breath, let go of my legs, and let out a guttural sound from the depths of my belly "ahhhhhhhhhh," and in that moment, everything I knew and understood about my body, dance, movement, and life . . . changed. My physical body turned into a flow of emotions, emotions turned into tears, and before I had a chance to know what was happening, my life came up from the depths and poured in a continuous stream down my face and onto my mat.

The moment flooded every crevice of my being. I was devoid of struggle, fear, or pain—it wasn't pulling on me anymore. I stepped out of separateness and into wholeness (as new-age-y as it all sounds) IT WAS BLISS. The experience was mysteriously invigorating and surprisingly ALIVE. I knew right there that I could never turn back and unsee what I just experienced. Needless to say my world did a 180 and my yoga journey had begun. What I didn't know was that it was about to change the course of my lifes path as I knew it.

Naturally, I took this new found experience and began seeking out ways to continue the feeling that I encountered. It didn't take long before I became a certified yoga instructor. Through studying, attending workshops, teacher trainings, and retreats,

I learned the art of feeling life through movement in a totally different way. Instead of feeling my outward expression in the world as I did with dance, I now felt a self connection to the world with yoga. It rocked me and I was loving it. I took key tools from well versed instructors who had their own styles and approaches to this mind-body modality, and I made it my own. Some of the teachers, Shiva Rea, Erich Schiffman, Jeff Migdow, Rodney Yee, and so many more had such a transformative effect on my life. They helped shape me and my choices in preparation to teach others this profound connection.

As fate would have it, I slowly moved away from a performing career, got married, started a family, and taught yoga as my main source of income. Although I was grateful for the ability to work at something that gave me great joy, and offer my students the experience I treasured so much, teaching five to ten classes a week didn't give me the financial security I needed. I felt caught in the cycle of having to put food on the table and yet wanting to feel fulfilled in my career. I was on the edge of keeping a job I love versus potentially having to take a job I need.

I don't do well with survival jobs ie: desk jobs. It's a slow death for me as an artist. I remember my mom sitting me down after I graduated high school and I was auditioning for shows in New York City. I wasn't landing anything at the time so money wasn't coming in. My mom, in her caring and loving tone said to me, "Honey, if you can't land a performing job, you

will have to find a 'real' job so you can start earning
money." Her intention was good and, in a roundabout
way, helped because, here's the thing: Lectures like
that either kick your butt and set you in motion to
succeed at something you want, OR they kick your
butt, and you let them kick your butt, and ultimately
give up on your dream settling for a job that you
don't want to do but has more financial stability. All
the demons come out and start convincing you that
fulfilling your dream, "Is too hard," "You're not good
enough," and  "You don't have what it takes." They
were out in full force that day during that talk with
my mom. But, for me, a desk job wasn't going to steal
my Broadway dream. I wasn't about to give up on
all that work . . . and I didn't. But my mom's voice still
reverberated in my head as I approached life as a
yoga instructor. And once again I was faced with the
"one or the other" scenario. It's a blessing and a curse
for an artist who survives on personal expression
while trying to make it in the world.

I was at my acupuncturist's office for a tune-
up during the winter of 2004. I was four years into
parenting and feeling very low emotionally. Life's hands
were getting tighter around my neck and I wasn't
hopeful about my future. The acupuncturist took out a
Young Living essential oil called Joy, rubbed some on
my heart, finished the session, and sent me on my way.
My initial response was, "Aaaand a smelly oil is going
to make me feel better? Yeah . . . right." On my way
home I noticed, through my skepticism, a subtle shift
happening for me. I felt lighter, freer, and like a cloudy

film was being lifted off me. Like I was awakening on some level.

This didn't mean I was a "believer" in essential oils by any means. The oils smelled good and all, and I had a good experience with Joy oil that day at the acupuncturist's, but it took a few more test drives and applications for me to really give over to the fact that a bottle of oil was changing things for me. A few months later I talked to my husband about our budget and my desire to "splurge" on purchasing a starter kit from Young Living. I wanted to get my hands on more oils to play with, and the starter kit seemed like a good option. With a little hubby convincing, I put the kit on my credit card, and waited patiently for its arrival. The day the oils arrived in the box, I could sense there was a lot of awesome about to be opened, but I had no idea just how much.

**SIDE NOTE:** Becoming a mother can create the need to over-protect. When you bring a child into the world, it can feel like everything is going to harm your new baby. The magnifying glass lens tends to be all you can see through. This is how I experienced new motherhood. So I was extremely vigilant about researching, going to classes, and educating myself to make sure this was the right choice for me and my family. After continually having life supporting experiences, it didn't take long for me to start using every oil in the kit for my daily household needs. But it was the oil blend Peace & Calming that first made its way into my yoga classes.

After careful research and everyday usage, I decided to bring it into my yoga classes that I taught. It's tricky with yoga classes, because students get very protective around their chosen instructor, the temperature of the room, how many people are around them, and smells. I valued my yoga classes and my students and I didn't want to disrupt their experience or cause a change in the environment they had come to be so comfortable in. So I did what was considered "normal" and walked around the room at the end of my class, during savasana, and asked if anyone would like a drop of oil to rub on their feet. I knew this was something they were used to and I wanted to make it easy for them to choose for themselves. I figured, it's the end of class and they can leave if they don't like it. But I secretly wanted to see if there would be a difference from the oils the studio had already supplied compared to the oils I had in my yoga bag, and if it would change the students' experience as much as it had mine.

Immediately after class I was getting comments like, "I love the way that oil smells," and, "I feel so good." I knew they were experiencing what I had experienced at the acupuncturist. Soon students began approaching me whenever they saw me wanting suggestions for supporting their health and the health of their family and friends. I was becoming known as the oils yogi and lives were changing because of it. I started bringing my whole kit to class so my students could get the full monty effect. If a student had needs, I would pull out my oils, before, during, and after class.

One thing led to another and with a little shaping and
fine tuning I created a class called AromaFlow Yoga
(cue angels singing). Students experienced greater
balancing effects in their standing poses with Valor;
I got feedback of deeper sessions of meditation with
Frankincense; enjoying pranayama longer with Raven
oil blend, and Lavender brought savasana to a whole
new level for my students. Things just kept growing
from there.

## IN THE FLOW

It's been about ten years since I introduced the oils
into my yoga class. The transformation of students'
practices, their families' lives, and so many other
walks of life have been deeply rewarding to witness.
But there was an added bonus that I didn't realize
would come from bringing oils to my classes. The
journey from my acupuncturist's office to now, as I
write this handbook, has not only offered a richer
experience in my yoga classes, but also has shown
me a financial freedom and security that I never knew
was possible through sharing the oils.

Since that time I have grown a Platinum tribe of
3,000 Young Living Luminaires. I spend my winters
on the beach in Florida while maintaining the same
income. The AromaFlow Yoga classes I was teaching
created balance in my life. Where once I would wake
up in a panic about securing my family's future, I
now feel the relief of supporting my family. Spending
my whole paycheck on groceries, after a week of

teaching private classes, gym yoga classes, YMCA yoga classes, yoga studio classes, and not having anything saved away for my son's college tuition or my retirement is over. I can teach whenever I want; run my own schedule, and live life on my terms. It's the most rewarding feeling to help people deepen their yoga and life experience through oils while maintaining my own life's equilibrium. And even more awesome, I'm helping other yoga teachers who struggle with the same conflict, free themselves from the bondage of an added survival job.

My purpose for writing this handbook is to change lives through practicing and teaching yoga with the use of Young Living oils. Whether you are in practice for yourself, or you are teaching in your community, the oils will deepen every aspect of your class. Deeper breaths for pranayama, more agility during asanas, greater groundedness while balancing, and a quieter mind in meditation. And what's more, the life of an aspiring entrepreneurial yogi doesn't need to end within the first year of being certified. You can grow your mind, body, and financial consciousness. No more working your butt off only to spend it all on one week of groceries. No more working two desk jobs while pushing aside what you truly love as a hobby. No more giving up on your dreams to travel, or take month-long vacations, or pay off debt, or save for a house or retirement, or have the ability to give to the ones who are in great need of your support. I'm here to tell you: You can do them both, love what you do AND make a solid income in tandem with each other, so everyone feels blessed. We all need to knock down the barriers to our rightful abundance, and allow financial healing to occur.

This handbook will show you how to integrate Young Living Essential Oils into a standard hatha yoga class. From there you can add your style and personal touch keeping it authentic for both you and your students. I'll present tips on how to bring oils into yoga studios, gyms, or any facility that offers yoga classes. Keeping it simple is the focus so you can relax around sharing from your heart, not from your need.

*Let's start!*

# The Essentials

# INTRODUCTION

Before we launch into a handbook about bringing oils into a yoga practice, I want to take a moment to address those who are brand new to yoga and have a secret desire to try it, but feel un-"fit" in keeping up with the yoga fitness frenzy. Let's make sure we start on the same page when it comes to simply "doing yoga" at all, let alone bringing essential oils into the mix. We all fear being seen on some level, especially if there is physical movement involved. And we all have the tendency to get caught in the ego's desire to be somebody else or prove our worth to the world around us. But there's something we need to clear up from the start . . . you don't have to be flexible to do yoga. You don't have to come from a dance or gymnastics background, you don't have to be an athlete, or look like a sports model, you definitely don't have to give up your belief system, AND you don't have to know anything about yoga to do it.

There are lots of stigmas around stepping into a yoga class or practice that it can be very hard for anyone to approach a yoga practice. So let's bust through some of those myths before you decide it's not right for you. Instead of coming toward yoga to conquer it with an already physically fit and flexible body, look at it like a vehicle to access your unique and unlimited body/mind potential. (Did I lose you there?)

Our culture made you believe that yoga is for those who can put their feet behind their head, or balance upside down for hours at a time, in perfectly toned bodies with perfectly shaped breasts bulging out of the latest yoga fashion. Hold the phone. That's not you; that's not me, and it's not real. The goal here is to take the smoke screen off the lens and look deeper into you, your students, and what yoga can offer. Whenever people tell me, "Oh I wish I could do yoga but I'm not very flexible," or, "I need to lose weight before I step foot into a yoga studio," I take a pause. It's disheartening to hear that our culture has coerced us into thinking we need to be something other than our true selves when approaching a 5,000-year-old healing treasure.

I'm grateful yoga found its way into mainstream, but it's up to us to keep tabs on what is being presented to us. Yoga is steeped in ancient roots, and it's accessible to every human on the planet. Here's why: the word yoga means "join" / "yolk" / "union" / "connect." Most of us see yoga as a noun, "Let's *do* yoga," "I am *doing* yoga postures." But I'm inviting you to think of yoga as an adjective, "I am in a state of yoga," "This feels like a yogic moment." Because the idea is connection, connection to something that allows you to feel and experience it, and the experience of connection is a state of yoga, a joyful and blissful, fulfilling yogic experience.

Does one *do* yoga? Yes. Can you become physically fit from doing yoga? Yes, yes, yes. BUT, if you go to a yoga class, or start a practice with the idea that you want to *do* yoga to get fit, you may never make it there, because like all exercise and fitness crazes, the bar gets set too high for the inexperienced to approach. On the other hand if you came to a yoga class to experience a state of yoga, then chances are you can relax around the idea of doing yoga and go for the personal experience, and not feel like you have to perform at an unobtainable fitness level. Out of this state of being, comes release of personal expectations, and with that comes a body that will respond organically, with it's own unique expression into flexibility and strength. You will have one of the most amazing experiences of your life. Right there on your mat. Trust me.

## ~ On the practice of yoga, the ultimate aim is one of self-development and self-realization. ~

Yoga is literally a way of stopping the chatter and pressing the pause button on all things that is your life, while connecting to you and your inner world through movement, and breath flow. It can be the most rewarding practice because it not only teaches and supports the body to expand the muscles and ligaments for greater physical agility and strength, but it also teaches the mind to expand, bend and strengthen when up against life's challenges. I know this sounds all crunchy granola and "pretty soon she'll be making me ommmmm" kinda talk, but don't worry, I promise you don't have to change your belief system or eat wheat grass. You are allowed to be YOU. This practice will actually enhance your current faith

and spiritual path. Contrary to what some believe
to be a religion, yoga is an ancient art and has been
practiced for thousands of years giving us all access
to a universal, all-inclusive philosophy of life. That life
philosophy is based on joining you with god, universe,
spirit, the divine, or cosmic consciousness. The choice
is solely yours. Oh, and we'll get to om-ing later.

Now, if you are a practiced yogi, and have already
found the value yoga holds in your life, but are curious
about adding essential oils into your practice, you
are in for a real treat. Essential oils will magnify the
experience for you and take you deeper into your
mind-body connection. And, for the yogi who is
already practiced in both yoga and oils, then I invite
you to pick up some ideas here and share it with
others so you don't keep all that awesome to yourself!

Whatever level you find yourself in, I believe you
will come away from this guide feeling energized
and excited not only about a personal yoga practice,
but also integrating the use of essential oils into your
practice and class for a richer experience. I believe
the two were meant for each other.

*~ The use of essential oils has the ability to enhance any
form of yoga practice and transport your experience to a
whole new level. ~*

For both an energizing and meditative practice, the
marriage of the two is truly worth exploring.

## HOW DOES THIS HANDBOOK BENEFIT ME?

For the inexperienced yet curious yogi who
might be fearful of stepping onto a yoga mat, and
for the practiced yogi who is looking to take their
practice to the next level, essential oils will offer a
welcoming platform and support system for checking
self-criticism at the door and broadening the mind-
body experience. It also benefits the yoga instructor
who wants to bring essential oils into a yoga studio
and offer a richer, more unique experience to their
students. The suggestions and instructions I give
in this book will serve every aspect of your yoga
journey. Whether you stream a yoga class on your
computer and follow along, or you step into a class
as the instructor, using essential oils in your practice
changes your experience. If, like many of us oilers, you
feel compelled to share the experience with others,
I've offered suggestions for you throughout the book
to help you. My hope is that you come away from your
mat wanting to share it with the world!

## WHAT ARE ESSENTIAL OILS?

Essential oils are aromatic liquids distilled from
plants, bushes, trees, flowers, roots, and seeds. Each
plant has hundreds of constituents that give the plant
its properties. Essential oils are far more potent than
dried herbs. The growing, harvesting and distillation
process must be very precise to each plant so as
not to destroy the valuable properties of the plant's
essential oil. If you go into your garden and pick
a leaf of basil or oregano and rub it between your

fingers you are smelling the essential oil of the plant. And while plants from the garden are delicious and healthy, with a drop of oil from the bottle, you are getting way more potency and benefits.

Did you know that one drop of Peppermint essential oil equals twenty-eight cups of Peppermint tea? Crazy right? Crazy good. Oils warrant our respect. You learn quickly when you pour a whole bottle of Peppermint oil in your bath water without noticing that the reducer cap had come off the bottle. Yep. True story. Keep in mind it didn't harm anyone, just made for a very chilly and uncomfortable sensation upon exiting the bath. Essential oils, Young Living oils that is, are a safe self-care system. Nature has an intelligence that has proven itself over and over again for thousands of years, long before we got here. There is so much to take advantage of in those little brown bottles that will support you and your students on and off the mat.

## CHOOSING ESSENTIAL OILS

*Young Living*™ is my choice for essential oils. After careful research, and ten-plus years of personal experience, Young Living Essential Oils came out far superior for me in my yoga practice. As with all things, you need to do your own research and experimentation to ultimately feel comfortable with the essential oils you use for your practice. But because I work with Young Living oils, that is what I will be referring to throughout this book.

I chose Young Living because they have been farming and bottling plant oils for over twenty years. They own nine farms in four continents, and continue to grow and acquire farmland while holding the vision to bring it into every home in the world. Young Living's "Seed to Seal" promise is unmatched. They never accept diluted, cut, or adulterated oils. To guarantee consistent quality, Young Living Essential Oils are tested in their own internal labs, as well as in third-party facilities, to ensure that they meet stringent specifications, exceed international standards, and contain optimal levels of natural bioactive compounds. The company makes you feel really confident about the oils you use, and your family's health choices. To learn more, visit www.seedtoseal.com.

Because of the high standards that Young Living has set in place, you may find that you experience the effects of its purity within minutes. And because of those effects, more people are becoming curious and therefore more companies want to get in on the action and create their own version of essential oils. Although the growing market has created an interest in essential oils, that doesn't mean you're getting a pure product. Big flashy ads may look enticing, but it's what's under the belly of a company that you need to look for if you want to experience the desired results you are promised. If you are an essential oil novice or someone who is venturing into this lifestyle path, step with caution, and do your research. Thorough investigation is imperative when choosing your essential oils source. Be sure to see the reference page in the back of this handbook for some resources.

## KNOW THE COMPANY YOU CHOOSE

I first looked at the company Young Living back when my acupuncturist used Joy oil blend on me over ten years ago. I did my own personal research to see if the company was the right fit for me and my personal standards. I even asked my husband to weigh in on it with me. He tends to ask all the legit questions when it comes to purchasing a product, especially if it is a multi-level marketing company, like Young Living. My husband is the biggest skeptic, and can sit for hours researching, reading reviews, and compiling his thoughts on whether or not to make the purchase. Together we found Young Living was without a doubt the best essential oil company to integrate into our life, family, and practice.

This was a no-brainer when we took our first trip to Utah and visited Young Living's Mona Farm and distillery. The family-like atmosphere and hands-on experience was key to our falling in love with the company. We saw first hand how the company treats their customers, distributors, land, and livestock. We continue to go back every year for Young Living's annual convention, and the love affair continues. It's vital to your essential oil experience to have the purest oils in your hands when yielding the results you are looking for. If you don't know what is in your essential oil, where it is from, or how it is grown, harvested, and distilled, then you don't know what you are putting in or on your body, or more importantly, what you are sharing with others. There can be repercussions, so keep it real. Something I make sure to tell my students before I teach any of my classes is, when I'm talking about an oil, I'm only talking about Young Living Essential Oils. Not the health food store brands or younger companies who saw a market growing and wanted in. Young Living's founder Gary Young set the industry standard, and the company continues to raise the bar on purity, efficacy, and scope of essential oils.

> *~ Study nature, love nature, stay close to nature,*
> *it will never fail you. ~*

## HOW DO ESSENTIAL OILS WORK?

I'm no scientist, but I picked up real fast the nature of how oils work. It's a little bit of chemistry and biology 101. Plants are from the earth and our bodies are from the earth. The harmonic language that happens when the two come together is primal and highly intelligent. The body recognizes the plant oil molecules as being made of organic matter, the same infrastructure as its own. This allows the body to invite the plant into every cell, like food, like a key in a lock. The plant oil and all its molecules then make their way throughout the body and, within minutes, scavenges all that is unrecognizable, and sends it to the dump, leaving the body feeling more like its optimal self.

It's important to drink a lot of water when using essential oils, so you can support the cleanup process. Just by breathing a pure essential oil, all body systems respond to its chemistry signal and the process of balance begins. On the contrary, with perfumes or synthetics the body can't understand the language it's trying to speak and works very hard to try to expel any foreign matter. This is why you want oils or any product you expose yourself to, for that matter, to be pure food for the body, otherwise we won't truly get the benefits we desire. That's the layman's version. There's a ton more to learn on the subject if you like getting your science on.

## HOW TO USE ESSENTIAL OILS IN YOUR PRACTICE

If you've never used essential oils, there are some wonderful resources for you to learn about how, when, where, and what to use for you to benefit. I encourage you to do some learning and exploring of the oils on your own first, so you can get familiar with the oils before using them in a practice or class. With that in mind,find a resource, like the person who introduced you to oils and see the resources guide in the back of this book for well informed materials.

It's important to note that the FDA has separate categories for topical and internal oil use, Young Living needed to label their oils to reflect these two categories; regular colored labels for topical & aromatic use, and vitality white labels for internal use. Same oil, but different labels (see appendix G page 71). I'll be offering both uses for each label throughout the class so you can play with the options.

Here are the three basic ways to use essential oils in your practice and life.

## AROMATICALLY

- 2-3 drops essential oil rubbed and activated between your hands and inhale
- 6-10 drops YL vitality essential oil in a diffuser

## TOPICALLY

- 2-3 drops essential oil on the desired area of the skin or bottoms of feet and massage
- Follow label and a resource guide for any necessary dilution directions

## INTERNALLY

- 2-3 drops YL vitality essential oil in a vegetarian capsule and swallow with water (add vegetable oil for any necessary dilution)
- 1-2 drops YL vitality essential oil in water, honey, rice or almond milk, or Ningxia Red Juice

Never use plastic bottles or cups when using YL's vitality oils in your beverage. Always use glass or stainless steel containers. Why? Remember when I spoke about the oil's ability to seek out foreign substances, scavenge it up and get rid of it? (pg 21) That's what it does when it comes in contact with a synthetic or petrochemical. Try it! Blow up a balloon and drop lemon oil on it . . . look out! Moral of the story, you don't want oils breaking down the plastics of your water bottle while drinking from it.

# WHAT YOU NEED TO KNOW WHEN USING ESSENTIAL OILS

Following are general guidelines. Be sure to ask your students prior to the start of class if they are dealing with any health issues or sensitivities that you should know about.

- Seek the advice of a trusted health care professional when working with any medical conditions, pregnancy, or nursing before using essential oils.
- Certain essential oils have cooling or heating properties. Use an organic carrier oil like coconut, olive, vegetable, or almond oil to dilute any uncomfortable sensations. Young Living has a vegetable oil mix called V-6 that makes it super easy to use on the go. Be mindful not to use water; it will enhance the sensation.
- Citrus oils may compound the effects of sun exposure. Limit sun exposure for up 12 to 24 hours after applying essential oils to your skin. Do not put any essential oils in your eyes or ears. If this happens flush the area with vegetable oil, not water.
- For bathing, mix essential oils with epsom salts before placing under running water.
- Always follow individual labels on the essential oil bottle and a trustworthy resource guide.
- "Colored" labels for application & aromatics.
- "Vitality" white labels for ingesting.

# ESSENTIAL OILS AND FREQUENCY

Albert Einstein said it best when describing all things in our universe: "Everything is energy." We literally live in a sea of energy. According to Bruce Tanio, of Tainio Technology and head of the Department of Agriculture at Eastern Washington University, the vibrational frequency of essential oils are the highest of any natural substance known to man. Oils entrain the cells of the body to increase their vibratory rate. Through the principle of entrainment the oil's frequency will raise the vibratory quality of the body. Good health actually has a frequency of 70MHz. The measured frequencies of essential oils have been shown to go as high as 320MHz as seen with Rose oil, and even higher with Idaho Blue Spruce at 528MHz. Essential oils' natural ability to enhance our health and wellbeing are without a doubt vital in our lives and our yoga practices.

Which leads us to chakras. Let's bust a myth or two here as well. Chakras, because they are energy centers of the body that are unseen by the naked eye, get met with a lot of skepticism. But, just because we can't see the energy moving through our home wiring system when we switch on a light, doesn't mean that that energy isn't flowing to light our home. Same goes with our own body energy. We do know, however, when our energy is high or low at different times of the day, but we can't actually see it. Like Einstein said, all living things carry energy, a life force with them. Chakras are those energy hubs we pull on within our own electrical system. There are seven of them. Here is a brief description of those centers within the body.

- **First Chakra:** The perineum (groin area) connects our energy with the earth for grounding.
- **Second Chakra:** The sacrum (lower back and abdomen) connects to our creative energy and the pleasures of life.
- **Third Chakra:** The solar plexus (where the ribs connect right below the breastbone) connects us with our power center, and decisive wisdom.
- **Fourth Chakra:** The heart center connects us to the energies of love, giving love, as well as receiving it.
- **Fifth Chakra:** The throat center connects us with our personal voice and truth.
- **Sixth Chakra:** The third eye (middle of the forehead) connects us to our intuition, innate wisdom, and spiritual life.
- **Seventh Chakra:** The crown center (top of head) connects us to the seat of the universal energy. It's an energy that is all knowing without pain, or fear, and we may only tap into on rare occasions.

There are a plethora of books and information on chakras. I invite you to go learn more about them and how, when out of balance, they affect our lives on so many levels. It goes much deeper than the bullet points I gave you. The point here is that when oils are used in tandem with the seven chakras, all body systems respond with extraordinary harmony. This too can be a wonderful addition to your yoga class or personal practice. (See appendix D for a chakra and oils chart).

## YOGA AND ITS FITNESS COUNTERPARTS

Yoga brings about emotional stability and clarity of mind. The practice of yoga makes the body strong and flexible in the process, it also improves the functioning of the body systems (respiratory, circulatory, digestive, and hormonal).

Yoga can be expressed through many forms, Hatha, Vinyasa, Kundalini, Iyengar, Bikram, Chair, and Restorative just to name a few. Yoga is now being combined with many fitness counterparts and becoming mainstream programs like Yoga Fusion, Yogalates, Indo Yoga Board, Zen Core, Boxing Yoga and many more. It's clear the value yoga holds in creating a well-balanced life no matter what choice of fitness you decide to practice.

## YOGA + ESSENTIAL OILS = BLISS

Like yoga, essential oils are thousands of years old and have been tied with yoga in ancient India. Early yogis used oils, or *attars*, to calm the mind and enhance meditation. When paired with your yoga session, pure grade essential oils can enhance and deepen your practice by accessing the body systems on a molecular level. The scents and applications of the oils are transmitted directly to the part of your brain that controls all the body systems giving the practitioner an overall feeling of wellbeing, balance, energy, and deep transformation.

## AROMAFLOW YOGA CLASS EXPLAINED

Naturally, after you have done your own essential oil exploration, and you are feeling eager to practice on your own or share it with other practitioners and teachers, use the following class flow as a guideline to help integrate essential oils at specific moments in a yoga practice. Remember to bring a wide range of essential oil materials and resources to every class you teach. Leaving educational materials accessible in the waiting area, or a separate room so students can learn at their leisure, can be so beneficial to their journey in essential oil use. The key is that you bring your own unique style to your personal practice or your class flow, so your authentic self comes through. (See appendix C for step-by-step AromaFlow class outline, and appendix G for Young Living's premium starter kit PSK info sheet.)

The following pages are a guided outline on how to teach an AromaFlow Yoga class using Young Living's Everyday Oils Premium Starter Kit (PSK). I offer two options for usage depending on the label of the oil you have (regular or vitality). You can adapt this class to your own personal yoga practice, whether you are practicing on your own, or streaming a class from the computer. But for the sake of clarity and guidance for those who might want to teach AromaFlow, I'll be writing this class through the eyes of the instructor. I will be using Young Living's Essential Oil Premium Starter Kit in class because for those who are new to oils, it's the optimal way to start. (See appendix G for info on the PSK.) Otherwise, you and your students will be swimming in a sea of essential oils not knowing what oil to use, for what part of your practice or life. It can be overwhelming to the newbie, so making it a simple yet amazing experience is what we want to focus on.

**SIDE NOTE:** Young Living compiled the most popular oils into one simple, easy to get started kit, so why not take advantage of their genius. Plus, with the kit, there is an added bonus of obtaining a diffuser, so the studio owner or practitioner can set it out in their room, studio, or gym to enhance the mood of the space and clear out any residual odors. This is much cleaner and healthier on the respiratory system than breathing smoke from incense. When your student or yogi friend purchases their own PSK, they now have their own 24 percent discounted wholesale account, and can come and go from Young Living at their leisure, without you as the middleman. You do everyone a service (yourself included) when you help set people up with their own oils, diffuser, and wholesale account so they can explore and purchase on their own.

Remember, keeping your focus on the yoga and oils experience and establishing an easy integration of a new paradigm in wellness is the ultimate goal.

# Class Flow

# GETTING STARTED WITH AROMAFLOW

You'll need to be prepared with a few items in order to have a complete and well executed AromaFlow class experience like your yoga mat, oils, mat sprays, diffuser, handouts, and music. (See a detailed class list in appendix B.)

**SIDE NOTE:** When sharing the many amazing benefits of the oils, we need to make sure we use FDA compliant languaging, and follow Young Living's compliance agreement. You can find it on the Young Living website under member resources. If you are planning to bring it to your community yoga studio or gym they will want to know what you have to offer. (For brief compliant descriptions on what to expect in a AromaFlow Yoga class, see appendix B.)

With your mat placed at the front of the yoga room, set out all the PSK oils in front of you, along with your spray bottles and diffuser. The oils come in a convenient box with a stand already built in for you to display them. Sometimes I like to use those little wooden tray slabs (you can find them at home decor stores), some have higher platform stands so they sit just off the ground making a more decorative display. Make sure you have set up your diffuser with about ten drops of Citrus Fresh oil in it for supporting an uplifting and happy environment. Leave the light glowing on the diffuser behind or near you, so everyone can see it throughout the class. It sets a comforting tone and offers cleaner air for the student instead of the heavy smoke of burning incense. You may not have access to an outlet, so be sure to have an extension cord handy, or find another place within the studio to display.

## INTRODUCING YOURSELF

Let your students know you are ready to begin. (I use my chime app called "Mindfulness Bell." It gives a gentle ding to alert students that I am starting.) Sit for a moment and welcome everyone. Introduce yourself and thank the class for opening up their minds and hearts as they take part in a new experience. Share your background and how you've come to know and love essential oils. Explain how it has shifted you in your life and why you want to share it with others. Define why you only use Young Living oils and the Seed to Seal standard of purity that Young Living upholds. Educate them on perfume oils versus therapeutic grade, and why only Young Living will yield the best results. It's also important to explain why you are using the Essential Oils Premium Starter Kit and why it's great for people who are new to essential oils. They are the most popular oils in the Young Living line to be used everyday, neatly packed in one kit, plus you obtain a beautiful diffuser for your yoga space.

## PREPPING YOUR SPACE WITH CITRUS FRESH. THIEVES. AND LEMON

Most yoga studios provide students with mats and equipment. Keep in mind they have been shared many times throughout the day, weeks, and months. So by the time you get to it they inevitably carry other people's energy and unseen organisms. In order for you and your students to clear the energy and the space around you, make a spray bottle of the Citrus Fresh, Thieves, or Lemon oils and spray your personal space, mat, or any equipment you will be using. Young Living also carries a pre-made Thieves oil blend spray that works great if you don't want to make your own. (See appendix E for mat spray recipe.) If you are using Citrus Fresh, Thieves or Lemon vitality oils they can be dropped in your drinking water to support healthy immune function. Depending on class size you can have one or two helpers pass around the oils and sprays during class so you can focus on teaching and keeping the class moving. This can be a good time to share some of the many other ways you can use Citrus Fresh, Thieves & Lemon oil in your life and the value these oils provide. It's a great time to teach the difference between "vitality" labeled oils and "regular" labeled oils. As well as "blends" vs "single" oils.

## MEDITATION AND FRANKINCENSE

As you start to settle onto your mats, demonstrate how to use an essential oil for inhaling. Ask your students to come to a quiet and comfortable, seated position on their mat and introduce Frankincense oil, the king of the oils. Show how to drop one drop of Frankincense in the palm of your hand, activate the oil by circling your palms together then close the eyes, cup over the nose and breathe. Pass the oil around or ask your helper to drop one drop in everyone's hand so they can experience it. Begin to guide your students into their pranayama breath work. While they are breathing you can gently invite them into their inner world. This can lead you into a visual meditation on the journey of the scent as it passes through the olfactory bulb and begins to activate the limbic and central nervous system. Share a little biblical history on Frankincense, and how this oil has been sought after since ancient times.

Explain why this is so important to overall emotional well being and ultimately meditation. Continue to guide them into a sense of calm and make them aware of the frequency that plants and essential oils hold. Start to take them into a mini self-reiki session where they use the energy of their own hands and the frequency of the oils to support any areas on their body that needs extra attention. Try this for yourself, quickly rub your hands together for about one minute, once you have done this, start to separate the hands slowly so they are barely touching, continue bringing them further apart and then closer together and play with the energy ball that you've now created between your hands. You are feeling your own body energy. Take your hands and slowly turn them toward your face . . . do you feel that? Now move your hands to a place on your body that is talking the loudest to you, that needs extra attention and healing. You can do this as long as you want, then turn the hands out toward god, universe, or spirit and send that energy to someone you know who needs some healing and prayer. Conclude by allowing the hands to rest with palms up on the knees, a simple sounding of Om, and eyes gently open.

**SIDE NOTE:** Look up the meaning of Om if you aren't sure or comfortable with sounding it. The simple philosophy around Om is that it's a "universal vibrational sound" or "vibration sound of the universe." The practitioner can become joined with that vibration and feel the universe as their own body. I like to think that it joins all the different energy that comes into class from students and helps to align them all so flow can happen more easily. I used to sound Om on my baby's belly when he was fussy, it would calm him down instantly. Next time you are vacuuming see if you can hear Om in the vacuum cleaner and join the vacuum in a Om session together. Ok, yes I probably took you one step too far. But I know you will get what I'm saying once you do it. If it still feels a little weird for you, I suggest downloading an "Om" track from iTunes, sit quietly for two minutes, eyes open or closed and listen. You are in for a real treat.

# WARMING UP WITH PANAWAY & COPAIBA

    After meditation allow your students a chance to move and shake their legs out and begin your warm-up section of the class. Introduce Panaway as a great oil to support the muscular system of the body and its amazing benefits. Introduce Copaiba vitality to drop in your water to enhance full body system support, or Copaiba regular oil layerd over Panaway to magnify its abilities. Talk about the safety of layering multiple oils during class and how to layer, by putting one oil over the other to experience greater benefits. As you begin your warm-up movements have your students tune into any physical discomforts they might be experiencing and demonstrate applying Panaway oil whenever, and wherever the body is speaking the loudest! Explain that this allows their body to loosen up faster and yields to greater range of motion making their practice easier with more agility. As you (or your helpers) pass around the oils, continue with spinal warm ups, hip openers, cat/cow, upward and downward facing dog and other movements that help get blood, lymph, and synovial fluid flowing. Continue with your own warm-up flow until you conclude with your students standing and ready for sun salutations.

# SUN SALUTATIONS & ASANAS WITH PEPPERMINT & DIGIZE

Once you are standing and you have your students warmed-up and ready for practice, introduce Peppermint & Digize oils. This is a great time to explain how some oils are hotter or cooler than others and why we use what we call a "carrier" vegetable oil like coconut, jojoba or Young Living's V-6 carrier oil to help dilute any uncomfortable sensations. (See page 23 - What you Need to Know.) Explain that it's common to use carrier oils when using essential oils on children or sensitive skin and why it's NOT beneficial to use water because it can intensify any uncomfortable sensations. It's also vital to teach about keeping oils out of eyes and ears. Peppermint & Digize vitality oil added to water offers a refreshing energizing experience, with many benefits for healthy digestion, or if you have regular Peppermint & Digize oil, apply it to abdomen, lowback, neck & shoulders or deeply inhale for five breaths. This offers the body the most profound digestive support and enhances the body's natural energetic rhythms.

Start in mountain pose (Tadasana) with
Peppermint hands cupped around the nose. Bring
your students into standing alignment and conscious
breathing. Ground the feet into the floor; wake up
the senses and begin sun salutation to start opening
all channels of the body. Whenever you finish a sun
salutation cycle with hands in prayer pose, you might
play with, instead of doing prayer hands, cup the
hands over the nose and take a Peppermint hit. It
keeps the mind alive and the body energy moving
forward. Offer different level options for those
who are new to yoga or aren't as agile, as well as
those who are well versed and more practiced. As
you take them through the sequences watch and
feel the energy and levels of the room, be sure to
accommodate all levels. Once you have completed
four to six salutations, bring your students back to
mountain pose and check in with how they are doing.
See if they experienced any different sensations.

Here, you can explain that sometimes when the
body starts to overheat, or exertion stimulates the
digestive system during class, digestion can become
uncomfortable (especially if you ate something
before class). DiGize helps with those discomforts and

supports you throughout class. From here you can move into standing flow postures (warriors 1 and 2, triangle, side angle, etc).

## BALANCES WITH VALOR

I'm going to stray here for just a moment with the oil blend Valor. Valor is not in Young Living's PSK. It used to be, but the high demand versus nature's growth time table makes it a hard oil blend to keep stocked. It gained a lot of popularity, and with a limited supply of key plants to create the blend, we are limited on how many valor bottles we can purchase in one order. But I bring it up because it is the best oil blend for supporting the skeletal system. Valor oil blend has a similar frequency as bone. Pretty awesome, right? So if you don't have Valor, don't worry, you can use Peppermint and Frankincense blended together to make your own balancing blend.

When you are ready to bring your students into balancing postures, introduce Valor (if you have it) and remind students this oil doesn't come in the kit, however it is very special for supporting the skeletal system that is why we add it to the AromaFlow experience during balancing postures. Pass around the oil and invite your students to apply the oil to their lower lumbar and upper cervical spine, as well as inhaling before proceeding. This oil is also revered for applying to the bottoms of the feet at the start of the day, however, because Valor has a carrier oil (coconut) in it, the use of Valor on the bottoms of the feet may make a yoga practice more challenging by causing feet to slide on the mat, so you may want to stick to applying to the spine and simple inhalation.

As you begin to guide your students through balancing postures, remind them that when we bring awareness to the skeletal and muscular system and focus on grounding our feet into the earth, there is a deep connection our body can open to with the earth. We can then become fully aware of gravity and our place within it. Remind your students about the rooting of a tree and its powerful rooting system in the earth. Balancing may become easier because of this gentle reminder. Once you feel grounded, emotional strength, courage, and VALOR take up residence in our minds, hearts, and body.

*~ When we invert our body, we reverse the pull of gravity and free up blood flow to all our body systems. The aging process is then suspended. ~*

## INVERSIONS WITH RAVEN

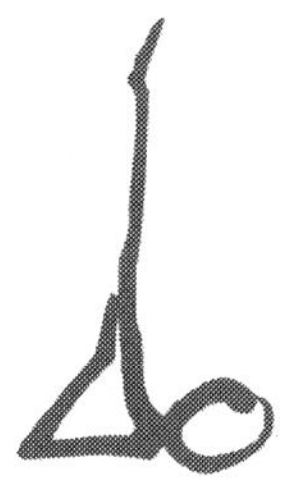

Wind your way down to a seated position on the mat, include any seated postures that you feel inspired to do. Eventually working your way down to prepare for inversions. Introduce Raven essential oil to help support the breath and respiratory system. During inversions our breath can become harder to access. Raven helps bring about feelings of opening for the passageways and supports fuller deeper breaths, even during the most awkward inversion. Have the students apply it to their chest, upper back, and cupped over the nose for deep inhalations. As you guide your students into inversions, give constant yet gentle reminders to breath deeply both in the front and the back of the ribs. Meanwhile suggest other ways to use Raven ie: during spring changes, or as support during winter time's respiratory challenges.

## SAVASANA WITH LAVENDER & STRESS AWAY

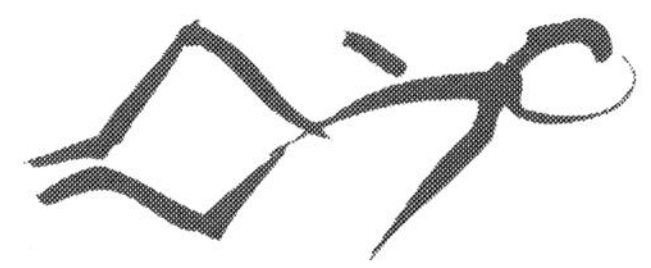

Savasana is the section of class everyone waits for in their yoga practice. It's the *creme de la creme* of the yoga practice, the moment when all the yoga postures and essential oils from your practice come together and integrate in a deeply, conscious, restful state of yoga nidra, (yogic sleep). Yoga nidra allows the mind to be fully awake while deeply resting. This is considered one of the most restorative forms of rest. This treasured time of deep relaxation can be very therapeutic for the student and can usher in a profound transformation for the practitioner. It's vital that your voice becomes softer, deeper, and more soothing to the ear, so students don't have to be so focused on listening but rather experiencing their body energies. This is the ideal time to introduce Lavender and Stress Away.

You can offer the student one oil or both, depending on their oils saturation level or desire to indulge. As you pass these two oils around, explain the benefits they hold for inviting a calm, relaxed state of mind and body. Suggest to the student to either drop Lavender or Stress Away vitality oil in their water to enhance a restful, soothing effect on the nervous system or apply the two regular labeled oils to the pulse points (inner wrists), neck, chest, and under nose. This is a perfect time to begin a visualization meditation. Starting with bringing their attention to their whole body and any tension they are aware of that they can intentionally try to release. Guide them to scan the body from head to toe and find the places that hold most of their tension (ie: jaw, tongue, ears, shoulders, belly, hips, feet). From here, turn their awareness to their sense of smell and the stimulation of the olfactory bulb and all the oils they have applied and integrated into every body system during class.

## ~ Experience self in silence. ~

Coming full circle from the beginning of class, have your students visually walk through the body following the scent into the brain, activating the senses, stimulating the limbic system which then stimulates all parts of the body, bringing balance and homeostasis to the whole being, emotionally, physically, spiritually, and energetically. Bring the students' awareness to the seven chakras (see page 25 for details on the chakras), the energy that pulses through and around them, and help transport them from their physical body to their energy body. Be creative with your visualizations, and guidance. This time of integration is so crucial to a yoga practice. This is why we do yoga in the first place, to bring us to a deeper state of self. Our mind is clearer, our body is buzzing, and our heart is wide open!

## CLOSING MEDITATION WITH TRANSFORMATION

This is also a very special time in a yoga practice. It is the state we all try to achieve in our lives, and yoga has offered us the portal to that state of bliss. So the transition needs to be handled delicately and supported with great care. While still lying in savasana, begin to invite the students to deepen their breath bringing their awareness back to the space and the sounds surrounding them. Guide them into moving their bodies starting with fingers toes and bringing both feet back to the floor to allow the lower back to rest fully on the floor. Have them roll to the right and press to seated position. Be sure never to rush your students through this process. Help them indulge in the moment-to-moment sensations that are arising.

Once seated and eyes still closed, explain that

you will be coming around with the final oil of class. Transformation. This oil blend is also not in the PSK, but it is such a perfect oil to help usher in any transformation your student would like to create in their life. If you don't have the oil, you can bring Frankincense back into the fold. Teach your students to anoint themselves with this oil on their third eye and crown chakras and deeply inhale. Ask the students to set an intention for anything they would like to transform. Invite them to search what aspects of their lives don't serve them any more so they can usher in change and that which will help to serve the greater good in their life and in other's lives. Once the affirmation journey is complete, guide the students into a breathing meditation for a minute or two keeping your voice soft and simple. From here you can invite your students into a final Om, ending your practice together by honoring each other with a spoken exchange of "namaste." (See the namaste meaning in appendix A.)

**SIDE NOTE:** It is important to take a moment to thank your students for sharing in the AromaFlow experience with you, and invite any questions, experiences, or thoughts they may have had during the time you spent together. Let them know you appreciate the feedback and welcome all experiences (good or bad). This will help you as an instructor to learn what you can do differently next time, or how you can continue the education of essential oils for your community.

# Your Signature Class

## ESSENTIAL OILS IN ANY CLASS

There are a host of great ideas for yoga and fitness classes. I used a generic yoga class flow as the foundation for integrating essential oil use into a practice, but essential oils can support any class that you enjoy teaching or taking. However, keep in mind there are hundreds of plants in the plant kingdom that make up essential oils, so it can be overwhelming for someone who is new to the world of oils to get started. That's why using the eleven oils in Young Living's Essential Oil Premium Starter Kit is so helpful. It's the best way to introduce essential oil use to someone who is new. From there the student has their own oils, diffuser, and account with access to a plethora of plant oils at a discount. With this solid foundation your student can venture into other oils when they are ready. (See appendix H for how to get started.)

All classes tend to have a warm-up, an energy peak, and a cool down, with the exception of a few specialty classes like restorative yoga. Since each essential oil has its own properties and uses, all you need to do is research and become familiar with that particular plant oil and it's unique chemistry, understand its many properties and uses, and apply it to each segment of your class. With essential oils you can enhance and create any class experience you want.

# THE IMPORTANCE OF SELF-CARE

Your body is your home, it's all you have to function in the world. If you don't take care of your mobile home, you are not able to reflect that in your life or your classes, physically and energetically, on or off the mat.

It's a constant focus as yoga practitioners and instructors, for us to pay attention to our health and wellbeing all day, everyday. Remember the oxygen mask on the airplane scenario and how crucial it is to help yourself first before your loved ones? Seems counterintuitive doesn't it? But it makes a whole lot of sense. We can't function in the world, much less teach a class if we don't take the time to care for ourselves first. And just like your external space around you needs to be prepped and in place, your internal space has the same needs. In order to serve others, it's vital to prepare our bodies so we can bring our healthy, full self to the present moment. It's not only a physical preparation but a mental and spiritual and intuitive one too. To be fully aware of your and your student's needs requires being fully aware of you. Yoga is a mind-body, energy exchange and essential oils in our daily routine aid in bringing balance to our life even in the most chaotic of times. Drinking plenty of water, getting restful sleeps, and eating organic vitamin rich foods are vital to living above the wellness line. If you find you are supplementing with vitamins and minerals, consider Young Living's supplement and personal care product lines. You will find it highly beneficial to overall health and wellness. Young Living infuses essential oils into its products so your body is receiving nutritional support on every level. (See appendix F for a suggested guide on implementing health and nutrition on a daily basis.)

## BRINGING YOUR SIGNATURE AROMAFLOW CLASS INTO YOUR COMMUNITY

Bringing an AromaFlow class to your community doesn't have to be a daunting undertaking in fact, it can be highly lucritive. If you are excited about sharing the benefits of Young Living oils to a fellow yogi, a yoga class, or neighborhood studio, consider exploring Young Living's compensation plan (see resources in back of book) and follow these suggestions below to get started.

- Start by making a list of friends, yoga studios, gyms, YMCAs, and fitness centers in your area as well as outside of your area.
- Send an email or visit the location with a generic flyer ready to give to them so they can see what it is you are offering. The flyer or handout should have a class description, a little bio about you, and what students will experience in a class, with a picture to evoke the potential experience.
- Offer different class options to fit the studio or gym needs, ie: Private Sessions, The 7 Chakra Class Series, Once a month AromaFlow Class, Once a week on-going AromaFlow Class, a 4-week series or more . . . get creative!

- Set a date or dates with the studio owner, or friend. Give yourself at least two weeks to market the class. Put it in your calendar and immediately begin marketing.

- If you're charging, standard charge for an AromaFlow two-hour class workshop is approximately $20 for pre-registered student, $25 for walk-ins. Don't forget that students are using your oils and you'll need to keep re-supplying so you may want to take into account your reimbursement. Some studios charge more, some charge less. It's important to accommodate their needs. They know their students the best.

- If you are renting the space and doing all the marketing and work, you will take the full payment from students.

- If you are offering it to a studio as a workshop and there is no rental fee, it's generally accepted that you take a 50/50 split with the studio owner. Some owners are more generous with a 60/40 split, others may take a greater cut.

- It's important to establish the who, what, and where when marketing the class. Ultimately it's your class, so it's your responsibility to make sure the word gets out about your class, to your friends, peers, colleagues, team, as well as the studio's roster.

- Make sure to get all your information together i.e.: date, time, place, who to contact if you're asking people to RSVP, cost, websites or phone numbers to call. Adjust your flyer for the studio space. Don't assume the studio owner wants to be contacted for ticket sales, always be sure to have that conversation. It makes for clean communication and no hard feelings if no one shows up.

- Market your class on Facebook, Twitter, Instagram, email groups, websites, Eventbrite, and by phone calling. This is the most crucial part of getting people to come to your classes. Don't always rely on the owner to market for you. However, ask if they would agree on sending out a notice to their contact list and studio roster letting their students know. Ask them to put a notice on their Facebook page, website, email blasts, and to put flyers in the studio. Continue to send out notices of your class as a constant reminder up until the date of the class. And use your Abundance oil blend!

- On the day of the event, *bring your own music speaker in case the studio's system doesn't work with your phone. You may want to have a Ningixa Red (Young Living's antioxidant juice) taste testing at the end of class for an antioxidant boost, and a sampling of the Wolfberry Crisp Bar (Young Living's snack bar). It's a great way to say thank you and give everyone a pick-me-up before leaving class.

- Always have a "Learn More About Essential Oils" sign up sheet for people to leave their name and emails so you can continue to educate them for years to come. And make sure to have your business cards on you with any additional information you can offer so people can contact you in case they want to learn more in the future.

- Be sure to find out what the studio owner is comfortable with when sharing with the class how to get their own oils. This can be a tricky path to navigate and you don't want to step on toes.

Yoga studio and gym owners are very protective of their clients and students. Many don't like the idea of an outside source coming in and "selling" to their students. Rightly so. They worked hard at creating a space where their students can come, let go, and feel safe in their studio. Keep in mind it's challenging for many people, including studio owners to see the ethical model of sharing oils that you and I see. There's a stigma around network marketing businesses. They are too easily labeled a scheme because the idea of "going for the sale" is at the heart of why many feel victimized in the marketplace, and network marketing has been pinned as the scapegoat. I was skeptical too. It wasn't until I saw the value that the oils had in my life and my student's lives, and how ethical this business model truly was, that I could fully embrace being comfortable sharing.

This brings us full circle. We are all working at some job to survive and feed our families. The network marketing business model that Young Living chose was based on family values and fair share for all. A philosophy that believes If you succeed then I succeed, your success is my success, and raising each other up for the greater good of all. Young Living is about offering a tool for greater wellness, purpose, and abundance. It's an equal playing field. I invite you to take a look at the business model you were raised on, where the owner is the person at the top who makes the most income, while employees make the foundation (pyramid), and are the worker bees receiving little to no income. That, to me, is the ultimate pyramid scheme. It doesn't give room for growth or potential for the employee. There's a ceiling on how far you can go, and as long as there is a ceiling, people will always look elsewhere for greater opportunities. There's a DVD called "Brilliant Compensation" by Tim Sales. It changed the way I saw teaching yoga, and how to maximize my efforts for my family and me, while serving others. Because of that paradigm shift, I am offered the ability to teach yoga for the love of it, while earning the income of my dreams based on my efforts. And even greater, is the blessing of watching other yoga instructors meet the potential of their entrepreneurial spirit, stand on a solid foundation so they too can support their family, serve others, and give wherever they feel needed, without the limits of financial challenges.

*~ Change the way you see things, and the things you see will change.~*

But like anything that has been taught to us over the years, it's a learning curve that takes time, education and an open mind. So it may mean you have to be a little more creative and release your attachment to an outcome when you approach a yoga facility. Understand their needs and desires for their students first and then shape your class around that need. The main focus is the essential oil experience.

Using an email sign-in sheet allows students to give you permission to send them essential oil education, or handing your card out after class for anyone who might be interested in staying connected with you in case they have questions, are great ways to let people know how to find you without any impression of selling. Or leave your info at the front desk so anyone who asks can be directed to you. Be in relationship first. Ask questions, be a good listener, and open your heart. Otherwise you won't know what their needs are and how to better serve them. Living by example is at the heart of a yogic life. People will be attracted to your joy and open heart, when you live authentically, and drop oils on them.

Namaste

# PARTING THOUGHTS

This book certainly doesn't encompass everything about bringing essential oils into a yoga class, and I'm no expert. We learn from each other and by experimenting with it ourselves. The purpose of this book is to spark an idea and elicit simple ways to bring essential oils to your yoga practice, class, and life. I hope this gives you a foundation to jump off from. Use it, take notes, color the mandalas, and let your creative juices flow!

I'm grateful for your participation in the AromaFlow Yoga class. If you'd like a one-on-one experience, look for the class on YouTube or Podcast coming soon. If you were inspired or sparked with a unique and different way of approaching your yoga practice, class, or financial future, I would be so grateful if you share this book with your fellow yogi or yogini so they too can benefit from the opportunity. I'm excited to see it support the future of our yogic community.

I'm fired up about AromaFlow Yoga classes moving out into the community with your personal touch. It's important to stay connected so we can share our experiences and allow others to learn and grow from those experiences. (See the back of the book for my contact info.)

The integration of essential oils and yoga can be a profound experience. Once it is truly integrated into your life, you will find it will transform who you are on so many levels as well as change the lives of those you drop on. It's the greatest gift when you can help others find balance in their lives.

I thrive on hearing your stories and testimonials. Please don't hesitate to share. I love feedback and hearing about all the lives that you are changing because of yoga and Young Living Essential Oils. We have just scratched the surface on the amazing benefits oils can have on your practice. There are so many more oils to play with and experience, so get your hands dirty and start learning. Get more and more oils into your life! But remember it's easy to get overwhelmed with how many plant oils there are on the planet, especially when you are a newbie, so start simple with the PSK in your classes and grow from there. Good luck with your practice and classes. Keep shining your light. The world needs essential oils in homes, studios, and lives, and it definitely needs your unique expression and spark.

Wishing you wellness, purpose, and abundance . . . and a well-oiled yogic life!

# Appendix

# APPENDIX A: NAMASTE'

You may have heard the word "namaste" at the end of a yoga class and wondered what the heck is the instructor saying and why are you making me say it. One of my students told me she thought I was saying "no mistakes", which got me thinking, that could work too (wink). Yoga is born out of an Indian tradition that we are all equal. This greeting with hands in prayer position at the heart, and a gentle bow forward in respect for others, is a way of saying "the divine in me, honors the divine in you." It has no religious meaning, it's just like saying hello or goodbye only with a deeper meaning and blessing behind it.

### Namaste'
{nah-mas-tay}
My soul honors your soul.
I honor the place in you where
the entire universe resides.
I honor the light, love, truth,
beauty and peace within you,
because it is also within me.
In sharing these things
we are united, we are the same,
we are one.

# APPENDIX B: SUGGESTED CLASS DESCRIPTIONS FOR MARKETING

~A typical AromaFlow Yoga Class begins with a short centering. From there you will be lead through a sequence of postures, with gentle pauses of essential oil applications, inhalations, and infusions, concluding the session with a blissful relaxation and meditation.~

~Learn how to integrate aromatherapy into your yoga or fitness practice and bring your experience to a whole new level. Awaken your energy source, deepen meditation, allow your body and mind to experience balance on a whole new level with an AromaFlow Yoga class.~

~Like yoga, essential oils are thousands of years old and have been tied with yoga in ancient India. Early yogis used oils, or *attars*, to calm the mind and enhance meditation. When paired with your yoga session, pure grade essential oils can enhance and deepen your practice by accessing the body systems on a molecular level. The scents and applications of the oils are transmitted directly to the part of your brain that controls all the body systems giving the practitioner an overall feeling of wellbeing, balance, energy, and deep transformation.~

## ITEMIZED CLASS LIST

The PSK oils come in a box with a stand already built in for you to display the oils. You can use wooden tray slabs from home decor stores if you prefer a different look. Set up your diffuser with about five to ten drops of Citrus Fresh oil blend in it. Leave the light glowing on the diffuser behind or near you. Be sure to have an extension cord handy, or find a place that will work best for you and the studio space.

## Items to have with you:

- Your personal yoga mat, with meditation pillow, bolster, blanket, block, and strap (can use studio props if they supply)
- Pre-made mat sprays (see appendix E for recipe)
- Young Living's Premium Starter Kit to display. This will make it easy for the new oiler if they decide to start their own oils journey (see "PSK explained" in appendix G and "How do I get Started?" in appendix H)
- V-6 Carrier Oil to dilute in case of sensitive skin
- AromaFlow Yoga Outline (see appendix C)
- Music ready to go on your phone, with portable speaker in case the studio doesn't accommodate the needs of your particular phone model
- Sign-in sheet to collect emails and Facebook names from people so you can stay connected
- Other educational handouts of your choosing for students to take home and read at their leisure (see resources appendix I)
- Extension cord
- A helper or someone to assist you in getting oils to people as you are teaching (depends on size of class)

# APPENDIX C: AROMA FLOW YOGA CLASS OUTLINE

Using Young Living Essential Oils Premium Starter Kit

## Yoga Mat & Space Prep – Citrus Fresh / Thieves / Lemon

- Promotes Healthy Environment
- Invigorating
- Yoga Mat Energy Clearing

## Opening Breathing & Meditation – Frankincense

- Emotional Support
- Pranayama
- Promotes Groundedness
- Respiratory Support

## Warm Up – Panaway / Copaiba

- Supports Muscle & Joint Health
- Soothes Minor Physical Discomforts
- Calming after Physical Workout

## Sun Salutations – Peppermint / DiGize

- Promotes Full Breaths
- Promotes Mental Alertness
- Digestive System Support

## Balances – Valor (not in kit)

- Supports the Skeletal System
- Grounding / Balancing

## Inversions – Raven

- Supports Healthy Respiratory Function
- Promotes Full Breaths

## Savasana – Lavender / Stress Away

- Promotes Feelings of Calmness
- Nurtures Peaceful sleep
- Supports Relaxation

## Closing Meditation – Transformation (not in kit)

- Empowers Life Change
- Supports replacing Negative Beliefs with Positive Outlook

# APPENDIX D: THE SEVEN CHAKRAS. ESSENTIAL OILS & ASANAS

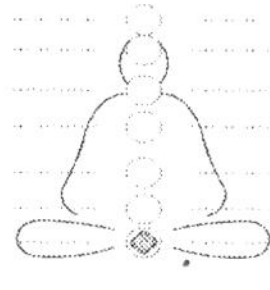

**1st Chakra** **Muladhara (Perineum/Root)**
Meaning - Foundation, Self Preservation, Belief System
Color - Red
Oils - Frankincense / Valor / Cypress / Grounding
Asanas – Pelvic Rotations / Squats / Pigeon / Goddess Pose

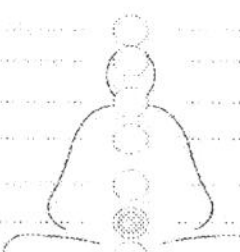

**2nd Chakra** **Svadhisthana (Sacral/Navel)**
Meaning - Relationships, Creativity, Sexuality, Yin Yang Balance
Color - Orange
Oils - Citrus Fresh /Peace & Calming / Orange / Clary Sage
Asanas – Cat Cow / Cobra / Bow / Dancer Pose

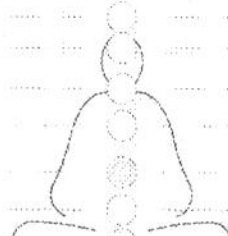

**3rd Chakra** **Manipura (Solar Plexus/Core)**
Meaning - Self Esteem, Power Center, Integrity
Color - Yellow
Oils - Peppermint / Transformation / Ginger / Digize
Asanas – Kapalabhathi or Hara Breath / Boat / Bridge / Camel

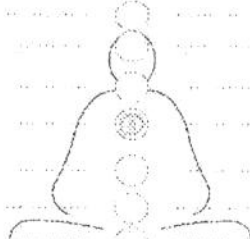

**4th Chakra** **Anahata (Heart/Chest)**
Meaning - Love , Forgiveness, Emotions, Giving, Receiving
Color - Green
Oils - Lavender / Gratitude / Joy / Marjoram / Believe
Asanas – Chest Fly / Child's Pose / Yoga Mudra / Fish Pose

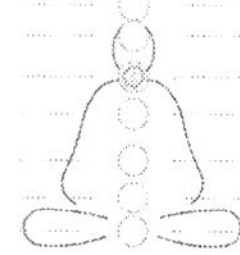

**5th Chakra** **Visuddha (Throat/Neck)**
Meaning - Self Expression, Speaking Our Truth,  Choices
Color - Blue
Oils - Thieves / Deep Relief / Endoflex
Asana – Neck Rolls /Locust / Plow / Shoulder Stand

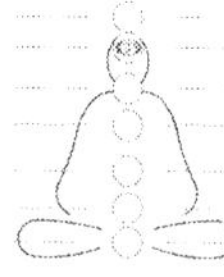

**6th Chakra** **Ajna (Third Eye/Forehead)**
Meaning - Wisdom, Intuition, Imagination, Insights
Color - Indigo
Oils - Frankincense / Sandalwood / Awaken
Asanas – Palming eyes / Standing Forward Bend / Eagle

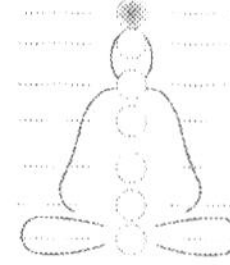

**7th Chakra** **Sahasrara (Crown/Top of Head)**
Meaning - Higher Self, Guidance, Spirituality, All Knowing
Color - Violet
Oils - Transformation / White Angelica / Cedarwood
Asanas – Tall Mountain / Rabbit / Head Stand / Lotus Pose

# APPENDIX E: DIY AROMAFLOW MAT SPRAYS

## Shopping List:

- 8 oz spray bottles (cobalt blue or amber glass*)
- Distilled water
- Salt (preferably pink himalayan, or epsom)
- Young Living Essential Oils (Lemon, Citrus Fresh, Thieves)
- Labels
- Small funnel (optional)

## Directions:

1. Add one small pinch of salt to the bottles (acts as blending agent). Using a small funnel is helpful here.
2. Add distilled water to 3/4 full to the top. This leaves room for spray nozzle without spillage.
3. Add 10 to 20 drops of the essential oil of your choice. Add more or less depending on your intensity preference.
4. Add spray nozzles, cap, and label.
5. You now have an AromaFlow mat spray!

* Dark colored spray bottles protect the essential oils from the sun and light, keeping the oils at their peak performance.

# APPENDIX F: ESSENTIAL OIL DAILY SELF-CARE

Here are a few suggestions to add to your daily self-care regimen:

## Mind

- When you need to take big deep breaths and feel your feet solid on the ground: Grounding, Breath Again, & Valor Oil Blends
- For a 5-10 minute "me time" pause in your day: Gratitude & Magnify Your Purpose Oil Blend
- When you need to step away from the "what ifs" and the "should haves": Valor, Present Time, Oil Blends
- We all need self-love and positive affirmations, take out your favorite quote or prayer while using Acceptance, Abundance

## Body

- If you are on the run and need to skip a meal: Essentialzyme-4, & Pure Protein Complete Meal Shake
- Add Vitality oils to your water for a healthier more vibrant you: Lemon, Citrus Fresh, Thieves, Copaiba
- Overall body wellness, especially when your immune system needs support: NingXia Red, Life 9, Longevity capsules, OmegaGize EFAs
- Before or after your yoga practice for when your muscles are talking back: Cool Azul Pain Cream, Panaway Oil Blend, Copaiba, OrthoEase massage oil

- Rest is the best time for the body to reboot: Lavender, Stress Away, Peace & Calming, Sleep Essence

## Spirit

- Protecting yourself from the negative world: White Angelica blend
- Giving your inner critic a break: Forgiveness blend
- When guilt guides your choices: Release blend
- Connecting all beings both human and in nature: Gathering blend

## Happy Day Recipe:

- One drop Valor blend on inside wrists, hold together
- One drop Harmony blend on solar plexus
- One drop Joy blend on heart center
- One drop White Angelica blend rub together in hands then sweep all over body

# APPENDIX G: PREMIUM STARTER KIT EXPLAINED

The Young Living Essential Oils Premium Starter Kit (PSK) comes with ten 5ml bottles of essential oils, plus one bonus oil, and a diffuser.

## 5 Single Oils:

**Lavender** – highly versatile for a relaxing routine, promotes healthy glow

> savasana, yoga nidra

**Peppermint vitality** – supports healthy gut and digestive function, respiratory support

> pranayama, sun salutations, standing asanas

**Lemon vitality** – uplifting, and fresh, elevates happy moods

> clearing, refreshing, uplifting

**Frankincense** – elevates spiritual experiences, maintains radiant skin

> meditation, pranayama, savasana

**Copaiba vitality** – very versatile, all over body system wellness

> warm ups, asanas, anytime for whole body support

## 6 Blends:

**Panaway** – after exercise for a soothing, stimulating experience

> warm ups, asanas, anytime for muscular support

**Citrus Fresh** – a refreshing, bright scent, diffuse in studio

> mat & space clearing spray, replaces incense for studio odors and setting the tone of the room.

**DiGize vitality** – a great after meal companion, digestive support
> sun salutations, asanas for digestion

**Raven** – supports healthy respiratory function
> inversions, pranayama

**Thieves vitality** – overall wellness, and healthy immune support
> clearing, promotes healthy immune system

**Stress Away** – uniquely relaxing and comforting
> savasana, inversions, meditation

Each oil bottle contains its own unique properties to support every system of the body, every day. Those systems are: the respiratory, digestive, circulatory, muscular, skeletal, nervous, lymphatic, endocrine, and more.

### Vitality vs Regular Labels:

Some of Young Living's bottles have a white label on them "vitality" oils which means they are safe for proper internal usage (see pg 22),. The labels are different, the oils aren't. Why? Just like when you go to the food store and you see coconut oil in the food aisle, you also see it in the personal care aisle, it's the same oil, but with different labels for different uses. The FDA makes sure you understand that not all products you eat can necessarily be put on your skin, and vise versa. (To learn more about the uses of each essential oil see resources in appendix I. To learn how to get your own Premium Starter Kit see appendix H.)

# APPENDIX H: FINANCIAL SUPPORT FOR YOUR YOGIC LIFESTYLE

I know your love of teaching yoga doesn't support the mortgage and the many bills you are faced with monthly, let alone savings for kids college tuition, vacations to Maui, or retirement. But what if teaching yoga offered you more than a weekly paycheck that gets used up on groceries? Enough to cover your monthly nut AND travels to your favorite place in the world? What if you could be financially free to practice and teach when YOU wanted?

Not all of us have an entrepreneurial spirit and wish to venture out creating financial abundance for ourselves. Some don't mind working for someone else and living within their set budget. But if you dream of traveling, paying off debt, setting your own hours, and retiring while still earning, Young Living's generous compensation plan can give that to you. The business model is such that YOU are in the driver's seat. It gives you the power to take control of your future and build your yoga business changing your life forever.

By being a Young Living wholesale member and using essential oils in your classes, your opportunities go beyond simply building a thriving business. You become part of a family of committed healers who all have the same mission, to serve others and build a healthier planet, while living a financially balanced life. I highly recommend Sarah Harnisch's book, *Game Plan* which offers key steps for building a Young Living Business. Be prepared to grow!

# WHAT DOES YOUNG LIVING OFFER ME?

- Generous Compensation: Young Living offers a compensation plan with substantial commissions and bonuses.
- Wholesale Pricing: Save 24 percent off retail pricing on Young Living products, and save even more with exclusive specials and promotions.
- Essential Rewards: As a member, you are eligible to enroll in their monthly Autoship Program and earn points toward free products.
- Awesome Experiences: Participate in unique events, experience Young Living's Seed to Seal® process firsthand at farm harvests and plantings. Take part in giving back on a global scale through the YL Foundation.
- Community: Enjoy a close-knit community of support. The entire Young Living family is ready to assist and encourage you on your journey.
- Education: Young Living provides ongoing health education opportunities through conventions, classes, and newsletters, to keep you informed and assist you in your wellness and growth.
- Recognition: As you share Young Living Essential Oils and start to expand and grow you will receive recognition for your accomplishments.

## Not interested In Going the Distance at This Time?

No worries. You can still enroll as a wholesale or retail customer and receive Young Living products. The door is always open.

# GETTING STARTED FAQS

## Why should I become a Young Living Wholesale Member?

Enrolling as a wholesale member puts you under no obligation to distribute the oils. It simply means that you get to enjoy the benefits of a discounted wholesale membership and save 24 percent on everything you order, forever. Young Living does not have any monthly minimum purchase requirements, contracts, or annual fees. It truly is risk free. They stand by their product and let the oils do the talking.

## Is there a monthly order minimum?

No. You do not have to order monthly in order to benefit from being a wholesale member. Once you order your premium starter kit (PSK), you are free to order more oils as the need arises. You are never required to order anything, ever. And as a wholesale member you will receive 24 percent off on everything you order.

## Do I have to sell Young Living products to be a wholesale member?

Absolutely not. Being a wholesale member simply means that you are getting your products at wholesale prices, 24 percent less than the full retail price. You are never required to sell anything.

## What do I need to do to get started?

To begin as a wholesale member, contact the person who introduced you to this book and tell them you are ready to purchase the Essential Oil Premium Starter Kit (PSK). The same kit we used in class. It is the most cost effective way to get the most oils right out of the gate. Plus you receive a diffuser to use in class or at home! And it will serve as your demo kit when you teach your classes. Use your friend's member number when enrolling on Young Living's website www.youngliving.com so you have a built-in support system and you bless their lives at the same time. If you don't have a direct source to support you, see all my contact info at the end of the book or visit susansantoromartz.com so you are guided in the right direction. Be sure to keep your enrollment password, pin, and member number because, guaranteed you'll be going back for more and others will ask you where you got your oils and how they can get their own, and you'll want to be ready with your member number to show them how to get started too.

## When You Keep Coming Back for More

When you find your love for Young Living Essential Oils is growing and you become interested in trying other oils and products but don't want to over do it on spending, Young Living offers a program called Essential Rewards. The program rewards those of us who are actively dedicated to our health, greening our home, personal care products, and wellness products and are using the Young Living store as our source.

Buying a little every month instead of splurging helps you save in the long run. On the Essential Rewards program, when you purchase a minimum of $50 or more each month, you earn points back on free product. You pay less on shipping, and can change your order every month. It's the most economical way to support your wellness.

## YOUNG LIVING ESSENTIAL REWARDS PROGRAM

- No cost to sign up
- 50pv minimum order per month
- Earn free product on ALL Essential Rewards orders
- Pay less on shipping
- Access to exclusive kits, sales, and promotions
- Change your order every month
- Change the date if you need
- Cancel anytime

# APPENDIX I: RESOURCES

## Books

***Essential Oils Desk Reference***, Life Science Publishing
A compilation of properties and capabilities of essential oils. Includes a directory of single oils, blends and personal usage.

***Chemistry Of Essential Oils Made Simple***, by Dr. David Stewart Ph.D. D.N.M.
Provides a fundamental look at the why and how essential oils work in the body.

***Chemistry Of Essential Oils Made Even Simpler***, by Michelle M Truman Ed. D.
A distillation of the seminal book *Chemistry of Essential Oils Made Simple.* This book breaks down chemistry in simpler terms.

***Rediscovering Nature's Essentials***, by Dr. Amanda L. Lukes DC
A simplified Essential Oils Desk Reference with a "Body System Approach" to EO use.

***Inner Transformations Using Essential Oils***, by Dr. LeAnne Deardeuff
Supporting the detoxification of the body.

***D. Gary Young***, by Mary Young
Gary Young's journey of bringing essential oil use to the US. His powerful experiences and personal transformations will inspire you.

***Releasing Emotional Patterns With Essential Oils***, by Carolyn L. Mein, D.C.
> Guidelines on working with the emotional body and frequency's using essential oils.

***AromaFreedom Technique***, by Dr. Benjamin Perkus
> Using essential oils to transform your emotions and realize your heart's desire.

***Essentially Fit***, by Adam Ringham
> Protocols for essential oil use to help support fitness and weight loss management.

***AromaYoga***, by Tracey Griffith and Ashley Turner
> More on how to integrate essential oils into your yoga practice.

***The 4 Year Career***, by Richard Bliss Brooke
> Learn how ordinary people created extraordinary lives through the business model of network marketing.

***Game Plan***, by Sarah Harnisch
> Tips and strategies for growing a Young Living business.

***Driven For Success***, by Jake Dempsey
> Road map to Young Living's compensation plan.

***Brilliant Compensation DVD*** by Tim Sales
> Shift the paradigm of how you leverage your efforts with your gains.

***Rise of The Entrpreneur DVD*** by Eric Worre
The search for a better way. Change the way you
view work and wealth.


## Apps For Smart Phone Access

G2G – the Essential Oil Go To Guide
Reference Guide For Essential Oils
YL Oils
The EO Bar
Mindfulness Bell

## Staying Plugged in Online

Young Living's website: YoungLiving.com
Purity Standards: SeedtoSeal.com
Young Living on FB: fb.com/YoungLiving
Young Living's Global Educator: fb.com/ed.dailey.3

# ABOUT THE AUTHOR

Susan Santoro Martz is a JerseeG'oil born and raised, a Young Living Platinum, certified yoga instructor, former Broadway performer, and mom. Susan started using Young Living Essential Oils in her yoga classes ten years ago when she saw a growing interest from her students and fellow yoga instructors who were looking to deepen their yoga practice and share it with others. AromaFlow birthed out that enthusiasm and is finding its way into yoga studios across the country. Today Susan supports a team of Young Living Luminaries both on and off the mat. She believes that movement, breath, and essential oils are key to living our fullest self. With the assistance of nature's pure plant oils, we gain access to the spark that lives us all. Find Susan online at:

SusanSantoroMartz.com
Facebook: fb.me/jerseegoil
Instagram: @jerseegoil
Twitter: @jerseegoil